W9-AUA-558

WHEN I FEEL
SAD

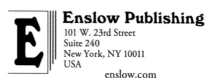

Amy Beattie

E **Enslow Publishing**
101 W. 23rd Street
Suite 240
New York, NY 10011
USA
enslow.com

Published in 2020 by Enslow Publishing, LLC
101 W. 23rd Street, Suite 240, New York, NY 10011

Cataloging-in-Publication Data

Names: Beattie, Amy.
Title: When I feel sad / Amy Beattie.
Description: New York : Enslow Publishing, 2020. | Series: My feelings | Includes index. | Audience: Grades K–2.
Identifiers: ISBN 9781978511545 (library bound) | ISBN 9781978511514 (pbk.) | ISBN 9781978511521 (6 pack)
Subjects: LCSH: Sadness in children—Juvenile literature. | Sadness—Juvenile literature.
Classification: LCC BF723.S15 B43 2020 | DDC 152.4—dc23

Printed in the United States of America

To Our Readers: We have done our best to make sure all websites in this book were active and appropriate when we went to press. However, the author and the publisher have no control over and assume no liability for the material available on those websites or on any websites they may link to. Any comments or suggestions can be sent by email to customerservice@enslow.com.

Photo Credits: Cover Tono Balaguer/Shutterstock.com; cover, p. 1 (emoji) Cosmic_Design/Shutterstock.com; pp. 4, 5 Blue Planet Studio/Shutterstock.com; pp. 6, 7, 8, 9 SaMBa/Shutterstock.com; pp. 10, 11 Bosnian/Shutterstock.com; pp. 12, 13 George Rudy/Shutterstock.com; pp. 14, 16 Veja/Shutterstock.com; p. 15 Spotmatik Ltd/Shutterstock.com; p. 17 James Steidl/Shutterstock.com; pp. 18, 19 Mikael Damkier/Shutterstock.com; p. 19 SewCream/Shutterstock.com; pp. 20, 21 Steve Debenport/E+/Getty Images; pp. 22, 23 unguryanu/Shutterstock.com.

Contents

I feel sad when no one will play with me.

I see someone else sitting alone. I ask her if I can read with her. Reading is more fun when we are together.

I feel sad when my sister is mean to me.

I want her to leave me alone. I do not want to hear her call me names.

My mom tells me to take a deep **breath**. She counts to ten as I breathe. Then she says my sister and I should talk together.

My sister says she is sorry. I ask her not to do it again. We agree not to call each other names.

I feel sad when my friend moves far away.

I write him a letter. I ask him about his new school and friends. He writes back. He says he misses me, too. We decide to keep writing.

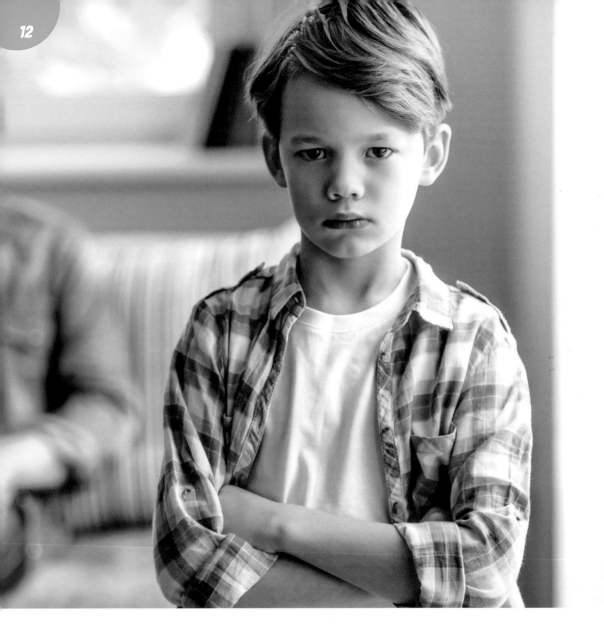

I feel sad when I lose my favorite toy car. The car was blue. Blue is my favorite color.

I miss my blue car. I play with my other cars.
They are fun to play with, too.

I feel sad when my grandpa is in the **hospital**.

I cannot visit him because he needs to rest. I do not know when I will see him again.

I make Grandpa a card. I tell him I miss him. I hope he feels better soon.

My mommy says he still feels very sick. But my card makes him smile.

I feel sad when I see a person without a home.

What if I did not have a home? I hope someone would help me. I want to help people who do not have homes.

My daddy tells me about the soup kitchen. People who are hungry go there. They get a free meal. We decide to **volunteer**.

We visit the soup kitchen. We serve food. I like helping people.

Lots of things make me feel sad. Other people have sad feelings, too.

I can often do something to help. Sometimes it is something small. That makes me feel better.

Words to Know

breath Air taken in through the nose or mouth.

hospital A place where sick people go for doctors to take care of them.

volunteer To help without pay.

Index